WACKY INSULTS and TERRIBLE JOKES

by JOSEPH ROSENBLOOM

PICTURES by SANDY HOFFMAN

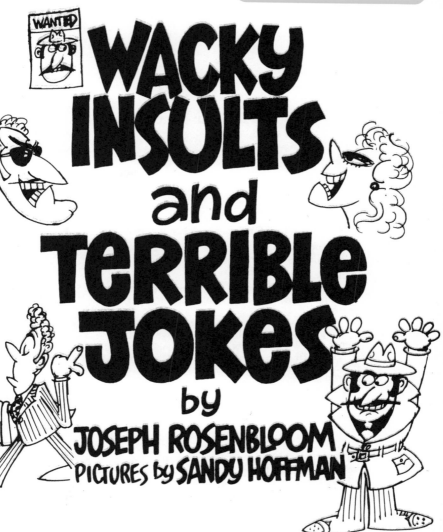

Sterling Publishing Co., Inc.   New York

To Adam Nierenberg

Library of Congress Cataloging in Publication Data

Rosenbloom, Joseph.
    Wacky insults & terrible jokes.

    Includes index.
    Summary: A collection of insults and insult jokes,
including verses, sick jokes, riddles, classics, and
new quips.
    1. Invective—Anecdotes, facetiae, satire, etc.
2. Wit and humor, Juvenile. [1. Invective—Wit and
humor. 2. Wit and humor] I. Hoffman, Sanford, ill.
II. Title. III. Title: Wacky insults and terrible jokes.
PN6231.I65R56 1983   818'.5402   83-4718
ISBN 0-8069-4674-1
ISBN 0-8069-4675-X (lib. bdg.)

ISBN 0-8069-7992-5 (paper)

Published by Sterling Publishing Co., Inc.
387 Park Avenue South, New York, N.Y. 10016
Distributed in Canada by Sterling Publishing
% Canadian Manda Group, P.O. Box 920, Station U
Toronto, Ontario, Canada M8Z 5P9
Distributed in Great Britain and Europe by Cassell PLC
Artillery House, Artillery Row, London SW1P 1RT, England
Distributed in Australia by Capricorn Ltd.
P.O. Box 665, Lane Cove, NSW 2066
Manufactured in the United States of America

First Paperback Printing, 1985

Contents

Books by Joseph Rosenbloom

Bananas Don't Grow on Trees
Biggest Riddle Book in the World
Daffy Definitions
Doctor Knock-Knock's Official Knock-Knock
  Dictionary
Funny Insults & Snappy Put-Downs
Gigantic Joke Book
How Do You Make an Elephant Laugh?
Looniest Limerick Book in the World
Mad Scientist
Monster Madness
Official Wild West Joke Book
Polar Bears Like It Hot
Ridiculous Nicholas Pet Riddles
Ridiculous Nicholas Riddle Book
Silly Verse (and Even Worse)

1
Signing In

"Can you give me a room and bath?"
    "I can give you a room, but you'll have to take your own bath."

"This place isn't fit for a dog."
    "Yes, it is— come right in!"

"My, but the flies are thick around here."
    "Well, you're not so bright yourself."

It takes all kinds of people to make up this world—too bad you're not one of them.

"What kind of idiot do you think I am?"
    "I don't know. What other kinds are there?"

You'd better keep your mouth shut. You don't want what's left of your brains to trickle out.

"What walks, talks, sleeps, eats, and still is dead?"
   "What?"
"You."

Please meet me at the pool. I'd like to give you drowning lessons.

"It seems to me I've seen your face some-
where before."
   "How odd."
"Yes, it certainly is."

"I suppose you think I'm a perfect idiot?"
   "No, no one is perfect."

"I have an idea."
   "Your luck is improving."

PORTER: Carry your bag,
   sir?
MAN: No, let her walk.

   "Did the mudpack help
   your wife's
   appearance?"
      "It did for a few
      days, but then it fell
      off."

No one can fool you—
you're too ignorant.

Use tact—fathead!

What you lack in intelligence, you make up for in stupidity.

"Did you fill in that blank yet?"
"What blank?"
"The one between your ears."

"When I was young, my mother used to say that if I made ugly faces, my face would stay that way forever."
"She was right."

"I'm sorry I lost my head."
"Well, don't worry about it. You still have the other one."

"Can you tell when someone is lying?"
"Yes, usually."
"Well, allow me to say it's been a pleasure meeting you."

Why don't you do like
a locomotive and make
tracks?

"Why don't you answer me?"
   "I did. I shook my head."
"You don't expect me to hear it rattle from
here, do you?"

"How is your health these days?"
   "I sleep soundly and eat like a horse."
"Please leave your manners out of this!"

"Did you fall down the elevator shaft?"
   "No, I was sitting here and they built it
around me."

"I guess we all just live and learn."
   "No, you just live."

"How are you doing?"
  "As well as can be expected."
"Pretty bad, eh?"

"What did you have in mind?"
  "Nothing."
"Ah, as usual, I see."

"What time is it?"
  "Sorry, but my watch is on the bum."
"I know that—but what time is it?"

Are you really leaving or are you only trying
to brighten my day?

"Please call me a taxi."
  "Okay, you're a taxi. But to tell you the
  truth, you look more like a two-ton truck."

2
May I Help You?

"The way you dress will never go out of style."

"Why, thank you."

"It will look just as terrible year after year."

"I just came from the beauty parlor."

"What's the matter, weren't they open?"

"I didn't come here to be insulted."

"Oh? Where do you usually go?"

"I earn a living by my wits."
  "Well, half a living is better than none."

"I'm not myself today."
  "Yes, and I noticed the improvement right away."

"I used to think . . ."
  "What made you stop?"

"What nice hands you have."
   "My hands are soft because I wear gloves
   at night."
"And do you also sleep with your hat on?"

"I've played the piano for years—on and
off."
   "What was the problem—slippery stool?"

You remind me of yesterday's coffee—bitter
and cold.

You are living proof
that wisdom doesn't
come with age.

Why don't you go
back to where you
came from—if they'll
still take you?

"I just flew in from
Europe."
   "Your arms must
   be tired."

"Someone once told me always to be myself."
"Well, you couldn't have gotten worse advice."

"You shouldn't make fun of my looks. All human beings are made in the same mold."
"Yes, but some are moldier than others."

"Was your boss angry when you told him you were going to quit next week?"
"He sure was. He thought it was this week."

"My fiancé says I'm the prettiest and most interesting girl he's ever met."
"And you'll trust yourself for life to a liar like that?"

Your face reminds
me of a movie
star—Lassie.

Some people grow
up and spread
cheer. You just
grew up and
spread.

"I'd like to find a dress to match my eyes."
   "Sorry, we don't carry bloodshot dresses."

"Who do you think you're talking to?"
   "How many guesses do I get?"

"Do you think I'm a fool?"
   "No, but what's my opinion against thou-
sands of others?"

Why don't you go to a tailor and have a fit?

"I remember when I was a mere child . . ."
"Wow, what a memory!"

"Did you notice I dropped some weight this summer?"
"From the looks of your knees, you didn't drop it far enough."

"Don't you think I look like a slender birch?"
"No, you look more like a knotty pine."

"Whenever I'm in the dumps, I buy new clothes."
"So—that's where you get them!"

Your clothes are so loud, they should come with a volume control.

"When is feeding time at the zoo?"
   "One o'clock. If you hurry, you can still
   get a bite."

"Goodbye."
   "You've already said goodbye twice."
"It's always a pleasure to say goodbye to
you."

3
Karate Chops

"Say, who do you think you're shoving?"
   "I don't know—what's your name?",

"I'm a self-made man."
   "I accept your apology."

You're so nervous, you keep coffee awake.

"Hi, Tom-ASS, how are you?"
   "I'm fine, Sam-MULE, and how are you?"

"My great-grandfather fought with General Lee; my grandfather fought with the British; and my father fought with the Americans."
"Your family can't get along with anybody, can they?"

There's a good reason why you think the world is against you—it is.

Your little mind must be lonesome, rolling around in such an empty head.

"Where do
you bathe?"
    "In the
    spring."
"I didn't ask
you when, I
asked you
where."

"I throw
myself into
everything I
do."
    "Why don't
    you go out and find a deep hole?"

When I look at you, I wonder what Mother
Nature had in mind.

"If I had a face like yours, I'd put it on a
wall and throw a brick at it."
    "If I had a face like *yours*, I'd put it on a
    brick and throw a wall at it."

You're so stupid, you think you have to stand
on your head to turn things over in your
mind.

Why don't you make like a ball and roll
away?

Why don't you take a deep breath—and blow?

I can't figure out what makes you tick, but I think it's a time bomb.

"I was great in sports when I was young. I had the body of an athlete."
   "Well, you still have the feet."

You must use gunpowder to brush your teeth, because you're always shooting your mouth off.

"I always aim to tell the truth."
   "Bad shot, aren't you?"

You could go out of your mind and no one would know the difference.

"You must be a terrific bowler."
   "How did you know?"
"I could tell by your pin head."

"Would you like to travel to unknown places?"
   "Yes, I would."
"Fine, go get lost."

4
I Love Monkeys, Too

I love you,
I love you,
I love you, I do—
But don't get excited—
I love monkeys, too.

Roses are red,
Violets are blue,
Oatmeal is mushy,
And so are you.

Sugar is sweet,
Coal is black.
Do me a favor
And sit on a tack.

Roses are red,
Violets are blue,
A monkey like you,
Belongs in the zoo.

I have you in my heart,
I have you in my liver.
If I had you in my arms,
I'd throw you in the river.

The rain makes everything beautiful.
It makes the flowers blue;
But if the rain makes everything beautiful,
Why doesn't it rain on you?

Roses are red,
Noses are blue,
Pickles are sour,
And so are you.

Roses are red,
Napoleon's dead.
Barrels are empty,
And so is your head.

Roses are red,
Grass is green,
You have a shape
Like a washing machine.

Roses are red,
Grass is green,
Your ears are
cute—
But there's
nothing between.

Roses are red,
Violets are blue,
Shanghai's in
China—
Why aren't you?

The roses are wilted,
The violets are dead,
The sugar bowl's empty,
And so is your head.

Good morning to you,
Good morning to you.
You look very drowsy,
In fact, you look lousy.
Is that any way
To start out the day?

I love to go fishing,
I love to catch trout.
I'd love to meet someone
Who'd shut your big mouth.

There are rocks in the ocean,
There are rocks in the sea,
But how the rocks got in your head
Is a puzzle to me.

You are mother's darling child,
Brought up with care and trouble.
For fear a spoon would hurt your mouth,
She fed you with a shovel.

Your father is a baker,
Your mother cuts the bread,
And you're the little doughnut
With a hole right through your head.

Roses are red,   Roses are red,
Violets are blue,   Violets are blue,
Umbrellas get lost,   Sidewalks are cracked,
Why don't you?   And so are you.

I wish I had your picture,
It would be very nice.
I'd hang it in the attic,
To scare away the mice.

Snow White gave a party—
The dwarfs were all there,
All except Dopey.
Where were you, my dear?

Roses are red,
Violets are
blue.
I was born
human,
What happened
to you?

Roses are red,
Pickles are
green.
My face is a holler
But yours is
a scream.

Your head is like a ball of straw,
Your nose is long and funny,
Your mouth is like a cellar door,
But I still love you, honey.

5
You Got Me!

"Sorry about the accident."
  "What accident?"
"You mean you were born that way?"

"I'm a bookworm."
  "Oh, I thought you were just the ordinary
  kind."

You must be the head kid on the block—the
blockhead.

"What do you mean—calling me deaf and
dumb?"
  "I never said you were deaf."

"What, in your opinion, do you consider the height of stupidity?"
"How tall are you?"

You're so stupid, I hear you tried to find the zip code for Lincoln's Gettysburg Address.

"Do you believe it's possible to communicate with dumb animals?"
"Yes, I can understand you distinctly."

"I've got a hoarse throat."
"Believe me, the resemblance doesn't end there."

"Have you heard the story about the dirty shirt?"
"No."
"Well, that's one on you!"

"Look at me
when I'm
talking."
    "I'd rather not.
    I have my own
    problems."

"What's today's
date?"
    "I don't have
    the faintest
    idea."
"Yes, I know
that, but what's
today's date?"

A crumb like you should have stayed in the
bread.

You're so stupid, if you shot an arrow into
the air—you'd miss.

"Did I ever show you this picture? It's my
father holding me on his knee when I was a
baby."
    "I see. He was a ventriloquist."

"I have a hunch."
"Really? And I thought you were just round-shouldered."

"Where do all the bugs go in winter?"
"Search me."
"No, thanks. I just wanted to know."

Have you ever thought of checking into the home for the chronically strange?

When you were born, you were so ugly that the doctor slapped your mother.

"You're lucky."
  "What makes you say I'm lucky?"
"Have you looked in a mirror lately?"
  "No."
"Then, you're lucky."

"My father is an Elk, a Lion and a Moose."
  "How much does it cost to get in and look
at him?"

"Your mother must have lifted weights."
  "Why do you say that?"
"How else could she have raised a big dumb-
bell like you?"

"You look like George Washington."
  "Is it my eyes, my nose or my high brow?"
"No, it's your wig."

"I can trace my ancestors all the way back to royalty."
  "King Kong?"

"A little bird whispered something in my ear."
  "It must have been a cuckoo."

"There are hundreds of ways of making money, but only one honest way."

"What's that?"

"Aha! I knew you wouldn't know!"

6
Out of
My Head

"Did you make up that joke all by yourself?"
   "Yes, out of my head."
"You must be."

"If a person's brain stops working, does he
die?"
   "How can you ask such a question? You're
   alive, aren't you?"

You might as well laugh at yourself once in a
while—everyone else does.

"Did you
hear my
last joke?"
   "I sure
   hope so."

"What's the idea of telling everyone that I'm stupid?"

"Sorry, I didn't realize it was a secret."

"My mind seems to wander."

"Don't worry. It's too weak to go very far."

"Want to lose ten pounds of ugly fat?"

"Sure."

"Cut off your head."

You're so mean you throw Mexican jumping beans to pigeons in the park.

You believe in law and order— providing you can lay down the law and give the order.

"I was driving to work and ran into a tree."

"That's something new. Sap usually runs *out* of trees."

"I heard you were at the dog show the other day."

"Yes, I was."

"Win any prizes?"

"You should always breathe through your nose."

"Why?"

"It'll help you keep your big mouth shut."

"How many lumps will you have in your tea?"

"None. I don't like lumpy tea."

"Keep still. I'm trying to think."

"Experimenting again?"

PATIENT: Lately I've had the feeling that everyone wants to take advantage of me.
DOCTOR: That's nonsense.
PATIENT: Really? Oh, thank you, I feel better already. How much do I owe you?
DOCTOR: How much have you got?

PATIENT: My hair is coming out pretty fast. Can you give me something to keep it in?
DOCTOR: Sure. Here's an empty box.

PATIENT: Doctor, I get the feeling that people don't care about anything I say.
DOCTOR: So?

"He's an M.D."
"Medical Doctor?"
"No, Mentally Deficient."

NURSE: Good morning! Did you take a bath today?
PATIENT: Why? Is one missing?

"Will this liniment make me smart?"
"No, this is ordinary medicine, not a miracle drug."

"You've got to admit I'm always trying."
"Yes, you most certainly are."

"I've got an idea."
"Be good to it; it must be lonely."

VISITOR: My friend was run over by a steamroller and he's in this hospital. Which room is he in?
NURSE: Room 104, 105, 106, and 107.

"Do you know what your one great fault is?"
    "I can't imagine."
"Right, only I never expected you to admit
it."

"Why do you wear eyeglasses?"
    "Because my eyes are weak."
"Have you thought about wearing a glass
hat?"

"Your feet are like your voice."
    "How's that?"
"Both are flat."

"There were eight morons: do, re, fa, so, la,
ti, do"
    "Hey, what about *mi*?"
"Sorry, I forgot about you."

"I hear you were run over by a train and lost
both your legs. How do you feel?"
    "Oh, I can't kick."

"He's played his last practical joke."
    "How so?"
"Just before he died, he left his brain to sci-
ence."

"The doctor asked me to cross my legs and he hit me on the knee to test my reflexes."
  "Did it work?"
"I'll say. I kicked him in the teeth."

CUSTOMER: Will you give me something for my head?
PHARMACIST: I wouldn't take it as a gift.

7
Hey, Waiter!

CUSTOMER: Waiter, there's a fly in my soup!
WAITER: Don't worry, sir, the spider on the bread will take care of it.

CUSTOMER: Say, waiter, why do you have your thumb on my steak?
WAITER: I don't want it to fall on the floor again.

CUSTOMER: How do you serve shrimps here?
WAITER: We bend down.

CUSTOMER: Do you serve crabs here?
WAITER: We serve everyone. Sit right down.

CUSTOMER: I feel like a sandwich.
WAITER: Funny, you don't look like one.

CUSTOMER: This soup isn't fit for a pig!
WAITER: I'll take it back, sir, and bring you
    some that is.

CUSTOMER: There's a fly in my soup!
WAITER: What do you expect me to do—hold
    a funeral?

"You look
full."
    "How full?"
"Aw-ful."

CUSTOMER: Waiter, how come this sandwich is squashed?

WAITER: You told me to step on it, didn't you?

"Waiter!"
   "Yes, sir?"
"What is this?"
   "It's bean
   soup, sir."
"I don't want to
know what it's
been—what is it
now?"

CUSTOMER: What
   do I have to
   do to get a glass of water in this place?

WAITER: Set yourself on fire, sir.

CUSTOMER: Hey, waiter! What kind of pie did you bring me? Are you sure this is apple pie?

WAITER: What does it taste like?

CUSTOMER: I don't know.

WAITER: Then what difference does it make?

WAITER: I have boiled tongue, fried liver, and pig's feet.

CUSTOMER: I'm not interested in your medical problems. Just bring me a cheese sandwich and coffee.

CUSTOMER: Waiter, do you have frog's legs?

WAITER: Yes, sir.

CUSTOMER: Then why don't you hop into the kitchen and get me a doughnut and coffee?

CUSTOMER: Do you have pig's feet?

WAITER: Yes, I do.

CUSTOMER: Too bad. If you wear shoes, maybe no one will notice.

CUSTOMER: May I have a glass of water?

WAITER: To drink?

CUSTOMER: No, I want to rinse out a few things.

CUSTOMER: What's the difference between the blue-plate and the white-plate special?

WAITER: The white-plate special is ten cents extra.

CUSTOMER: Is the food any better?

WAITER: No, but we wash the dishes.

WAITER: Is the food too spicy?
CUSTOMER: Not at all. Smoke always comes out of my ears.

WAITER: Oh, I'm sorry I spilled water all over you.
CUSTOMER: That's all right. My suit was several sizes too large, anyhow.

CUSTOMER: I'm giving a dinner for all my
  friends tonight.
WAITER: Oh—you must be the party that re-
  served a table for two.

You look like you're walking around just to
save on funeral expenses.

When you walk
down the street,
undertakers must
come up to you
and give
estimates.

CUSTOMER: May I have a glass of water, please?
WAITER: To drink?
CUSTOMER: No—to do a high diving act.

CUSTOMER: I understand that fish is brain food.
WAITER: Yes, I eat it all the time.
CUSTOMER: Oh, well, there goes another scientific theory.

You could be arrested for impersonating a garbage can.

CUSTOMER: I have a complaint.
WAITER: A complaint! This is a restaurant—
   not a hospital.

Why don't you make like a diet and take off?

8
All
in the Family

My sister and I had a good time at the beach last summer. First she would bury me in the sand, then I would bury her. This summer I'm going back and dig her up.

"But, Mom, that isn't our baby."
    "Shut up, kid. It's a better baby carriage."

"What was that noise I heard before?"
    "My sister fell down a flight of stairs."
"Cellar?"
    "No, I think she can still be fixed."

The only trouble with your face is that it shows.

Brains aren't everything. In fact, in your case, they're nothing!

You may not know how to add, but you certainly know how to distract.

FATHER: The man who marries my daughter gets a prize.
SUITOR: Can I see the prize first?

MEDIUM: I hear the spirit of your dear, departed wife knocking.
HUSBAND: Who's she knocking now?

FATHER: Why does Junior have so many holes in his forehead?
MOTHER: He's learning to eat with a fork.

If I had a lower IQ, I might enjoy this conversation.

If you were twice as smart, you'd still be a half-wit.

MOTHER CANNIBAL (*to Witch Doctor*): I'm worried about Junior. He wants to be a vegetarian.

FATHER: Son, you've struck out so many times with bases loaded in the Little League playoffs, I may have to do something I don't want to do.
SON: What's that, Dad?
FATHER: Trade you.

He went out for the football team because when he was born, his parents took one look and said, "That is the end!"

PROUD FATHER:
My baby is
the spitting
image of
me.
NEIGHBOR:
What do
you care,
as long
as it's
healthy?

The young father was explaining to a neighbor that he had found a quick way to put the baby to sleep.

"I toss it up in the air again and again."

"How does that put the baby to sleep?" asked the neighbor.

"We have very low ceilings."

"Now, Junior, apologize at once for saying Mrs. Smith is ugly."

"I'm sorry, Mrs. Smith, that you're ugly."

JUDGE: Why did you shoot your husband with
a bow and arrow?

WOMAN: Because I didn't want to wake the
children.

JUDGE: Why did you shoot six bullets into
your husband?

WOMAN: Six bullets!—I must be hard of hear-
ing!

JUNIOR: Dad, can I have another glass of water before I go to sleep?

FATHER: What, another? This is your tenth!

JUNIOR: I know, but my room is on fire.

"Mary, the baby has swallowed the matches."
   "Here, sweetheart, use my lighter."

"I broke little Tommy of the habit of biting his nails."
   "Really? How did you do it?"
"I knocked his teeth out."

NIT: Our dog is just like one of the family.
WIT: Which one?

9
Exercising with Dumbbells

"Would you join me in a walk?"

"I'd love to."

"Good. My doctor told me to exercise with dumbbells."

"When I was born, they fired a 21-gun salute."

"Too bad they missed."

"Excuse me for living!"

"That's all right, but don't let it happen again."

"Haven't I seen your face somewhere else?"

"I don't think so. It's always been between my ears."

Just because you've been off base all your life doesn't make you a baseball player.

How much would you charge to stand at the wrong end of a shooting gallery?

If your head was an automobile gas tank, it would point to empty.

Signal me when you've finished talking so I can take my fingers out of my ears.

Why don't you introduce your mind to your mouth?

What does your brain want to be when it grows up?

My name is Cliff. Why don't you drop over some time?

Is that really your face? Or did your neck throw up?

Is that really your face? Or did you block a kick?

You're brighter than you look, but then you'd have to be.

"Do you know the difference between a piece of birthday cake and an old glove?"
    "No."
"Good, then eat this old glove."

The closest you'll ever come to a brainstorm is a light drizzle.

It gives me a headache just to think down to your level.

"What's your name?"
    "Pistachio."
"Pistachio! What kind of name is that?"
    "That's Pistachio to my friends—and nuts to you!"

"The mosquitoes are biting me."
    "Those aren't mosquitoes—those are gnats."
"All right—mosquitoes to me—and gnats to you!"

"That boat does twenty miles an hour."
    "Not twenty miles. You mean knots."
"Okay, miles to me—and knots to you!"

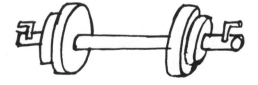

"I dreamed about numbers last night."
    "You don't mean numbers, you mean ciphers."
"Well, actually, they were zeroes."
    "You don't mean zeroes, you mean naughts."
"Okay, zeroes to me—and naughts to you!"

"If I stand on my head, all my blood rushes into it. Why doesn't all my blood rush to my feet when I stand on them?"

"Your feet aren't empty."

You're in such bad shape, you get winded playing chess!

The softness of your muscles is exceeded only by the hardness of your arteries.

I hear you tried to join the human race but flunked the physical.

Please don't tell me your name. I don't want to know who I'm hating.

10
Swing Your Partner

"Sheep are the stupidest creatures."

"What did you say, my lamb?"

Your timing is perfect—and so is your two-timing.

You're so worthless, lifeguards will only rescue you on slow days.

You have less backbone than a banana.

Your mind is like concrete—all mixed up and permanently set.

"Look, I went to college, stupid!"
   "And you came back that
   way, too!"

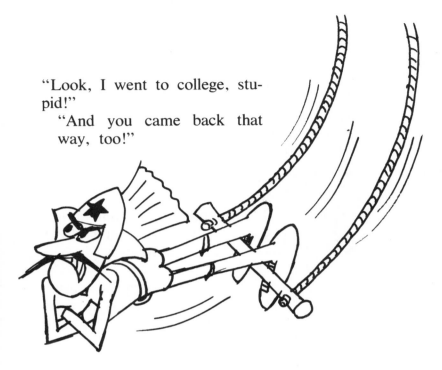

You're so prejudiced, you won't listen to both
sides of a record album.

Your mind is so open the wind whistles
through it.

"Do you think the saying, 'Ignorance is bliss,'
is true?"
   "Well, you seem to be happy."

Sloppy? You're a one-man slum!

"Do you know the difference between a sight and a vision?"

"No, what is it?"

"Well, I'm a vision—but you're a sight."

You're so stingy, the only road you'll drive on is a freeway.

You're such a miser, you won't even tip your hat.

"I gave you the best years of my life."
   "So what do you want—a receipt?"

You remind me of an unused roll of film—undeveloped!

Some people drink at the fountain of knowledge—you just gargle.

You talk so much that when you get back from the beach, your tongue is sunburned.

"I entered the face-making contest."
   "You did? Who won second prize?"

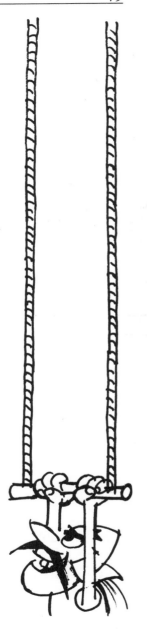

Your complexion reminds me of a peach—yellow and fuzzy.

"I've been at the beauty parlor for four hours."
    "Too bad you weren't waited on!"

You have such a dirty mind, even your shock-proof watch is embarrassed.

That joke of yours was so bad, you'd need a microscope to see the point.

"What's the difference between a sigh and a car and a jackass?"
    "I give up."
"A sigh is 'Oh, dear!' A car is too dear."
    "And what is a jackass?"
"You, dear."

"Do you love me?"

"Madly—I would die for you!"

"You're always saying that, but you never do it."

Here's a hand grenade—catch!

You're such a bore—people have parties just not to invite you.

"I heard a new joke the other day. I wonder if I told it to you."

"Was it funny?"

"Yes."

"Then you didn't."

You're the kind of bum who gives bums a bad name.

"I have my mother's ears and my father's nose."
   "They must look funny without them."

"That's funny!"
   "What?"
"I was just thinking."
   "Ha-ha! Now *that* is funny!"

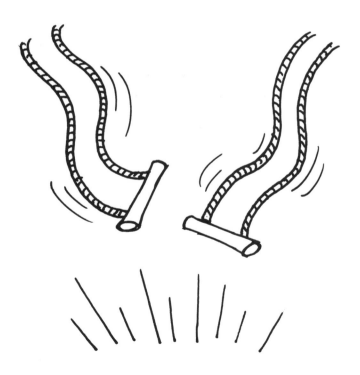

11
Quacking Up

Zeke, owner of the general store, was the meanest, most insulting man in town.

One day a man walked into his store with a duck under his arm.

"Say, what are you doing with that pig?" said Zeke.

"Are you crazy?" the man replied. "Can't you see this is a duck—not a pig?"

"I wasn't talking to you," Zeke sneered, "I was talking to the duck."

"There's a man outside in a black cape with a strange request," the nurse told the doctor.

"What does he want?" the doctor asked.

"Well, doctor," the nurse explained, "He says he wants two pints to go."

"You've got a very large stomach."
"Do you think I should diet?"
"Oh, the color's all right—it's just the size."

"Why did you wrap barbed wire around the bannister in your house?"
"Junior likes to slide down bannisters."
"Does the barbed wire stop him?"
"No, but it slows him down."

"When I was a child, I used to bite my fingernails all day. The doctor said if I didn't stop, I'd grow up to be an idiot."

"And you couldn't stop. . . ."

POLICEMAN: When he said he was going to step off the top of the building onto a cloud—why didn't you stop him?

LITTLE WILLIE: I thought he could do it.

MAN (*to GHOST*): How much will you charge to haunt my boss?

GHOST: For $10 I promise to scare him out of his wits.

MAN: Here's $5. He's only a half-wit.

The sawmill boss explained to the new man how to operate the buzz saw, warning him that under no circumstances should he put his hand near the blade while the motor was running. The first day on the job the man put his finger in the machine and before he knew it, the finger was gone.

"What happened!" the boss said, "Didn't I show you how to operate the machine?"

"I don't understand it," the man said. "All I did was put my hand out like this—oooops! There goes another one!"

"Doc, give it to me straight—what kind of shape am I in?"

"Let's put it this way: from now on you pay in advance."

"I don't care who you are, fat man—get those reindeer off my roof!"

"What is the first letter in yellow?"
  "Y."
"Because I want to know."

"Isn't it great to be alive?"
  "Yes. You'd be much happier that way."

"How's your nose?"
  "Shut up!"
"So's mine. Must be the cold weather."

Never argue with a fool. Bystanders won't be able to tell which is which.

"Everything you say goes in one ear and out the other."
  "No wonder—there's nothing inside to block the traffic."

Sign in store window:
HATS FOR ALL HEADS—SMALL, MEDIUM, FAT

CUSTOMER: I'd like some rat poison.
PHARMACIST: Shall I wrap it up—or would you like to drink it here?

"Excuse me, sir, but are you reading the newspaper you're sitting on?"

"How do you do?"
"How do I do what?"
"I mean, how do you find yourself?"
"Don't be silly. I never lose myself."
"You don't understand. How do you feel?"
"With my fingers, of course. Haven't you got anything better to do than bother me with stupid questions?"

"Thank you so much for saving me from drowning. I'd gladly give you five dollars, but all I have is a ten dollar bill."
"That's all right. Just jump back in."

Ali Baba went up to the cave entrance and cried, "Open Sesame!"
A voice called back, "Sez who?"

CLERK (*in clothing store*): Would you like a cuff in the pants or a belt in the back?
CUSTOMER: How would you like a sock in the eye?

"She has lots of gold teeth."
"No wonder! Look at her pan!"

Why did the little moron wear suspenders?
To keep his shoulders down.

"May I join you?"

"Why, am I coming apart?"

"I feel like a cup of tea."

"Strange—you don't look like one."

"I mean—may I join you in a cup of tea?"

"Absolutely not! There isn't enough room for both of us in one tiny cup!"

CUSTOMER (*in clothing store*): Have you any ties to match my eyes?

CLERK: No, but we have soft hats to match your head.

"How can one person make so many stupid mistakes in one day?"

"I get up early."

"I weighed three pounds when I was born."

"You don't say! Did you live?"

"Did I live? You should see me now!"

12
I'm Speechless!

"I'm speechless!"
   "If only you'd stay that way!"

"I heard
about your
wit."
   Oh, it's
   nothing."
"Yes—that's
what I
heard."

I thought my
razor was
dull until I
heard you
talk.

"When I got
up on that
stage, people
clapped their
hands."
   "Yes, over their eyes."

ACTOR: Have you seen me on television?
ACQUAINTANCE: On and off.
ACTOR: How did you like me?
ACQUAINTANCE: Off.

"That play I was in had a happy ending."
"Yes, everyone was glad it was over."

I liked the song you sang. One day you should put it to music.

"I quit singing because of my throat."
"Sure, the audience threatened to cut it."

"People say you're so conceited you write letters to yourself."
"Dear me!"
"Yes—that's how they begin."

The next time you get a toupee, get one with brains.

"What would you say if I asked you to marry me?"
"Nothing. I can't talk and laugh at the same time."

"Have you told your little boy not to go around imitating me?"

"Yes, I have. I told him not to act like an idiot."

AGING ROMEO: Hello, beautiful, where have you been all my life?

GIRL: Well, for the first half, I wasn't even born. . . .

You're all wrapped up in yourself—and you make a pretty small package.

You think you're a big cheese—but you only smell like one.

You have a very striking face. It should be struck more often.

"You should put a sign on your head."
"What kind of sign?"
"VACANT."

Your voice is so flat—it should be furnished.

"Singers (dancers, actors, teachers, etc.) run in my family."
"They should."

"I learned to play the piano in no time."
"Yes, and you play it that way, too."

"I've been playing the piano for five years."
"Aren't your fingers tired?"

The last time I saw a mouth like yours, it had a fishhook in it.

"You're half an hour late. I've been standing here like a fool."
"I can't help how you stand."

The only thing that you can keep in your head for more than an hour is a cold.

"How are you?"
  "Wonderful."
"I'm glad someone
thinks so."

The more I think of
you—the less I think of
you.

I've seen more interesting faces on clocks.

You hold your nose so high in the air, there's
always an inch of snow on it.

Your problem is that you're always trying to
save both faces.

Things could be worse. You could be here in
person.

"Only fools make absolute statements."
  "Are you sure of that?"
"Absolutely!"

Tight? You won't even perspire freely.

Some people are born great, some achieve
greatness—you just grate.

You ought to be an auto racer—you're such a big drag.

Whatever is eating you must be suffering from indigestion.

"I can't get to sleep at night. I've tried all kinds of remedies, but nothing works."
   "Have you tried talking to yourself?"

You could make a fortune renting out your head as a balloon.

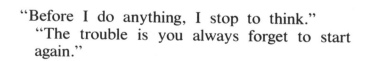

If they're not talking about you, you're not listening.

You have an even disposition—always rotten.

"Before I do anything, I stop to think."
   "The trouble is you always forget to start again."

"Am I boring you?"
   "No, just wake me when you're finished."

The only way you'll ever be wanted is to rob
a bank.

"If you work
hard, you'll
get ahead."
"No,
thanks, I
already
have a
head."

"She's so stuck up. She thinks she's so much
better than me."
"Why, that conceited, good-for-nothing moron! You're certainly every bit as good as
she is!"

My house is located near a lake. Drop in
some time.

13
Sick Jokes

"But, Dad, I don't want to go to Europe."
"Shut up, kid, and keep rowing."

"Daddy, why is Mommy so pale?"
"Shut up, kid, and keep digging."

"Mommy, are you sure this is the way to make pizza?"
"Shut up, kid, and get back in the oven."

"Mom, what's a vampire?"
"Shut up, kid, and drink your soup before it clots."

JUNIOR: Give me a cookie.
MOTHER: What's the magic word, dear?
JUNIOR: Hocus-pocus?

"Mom, I refuse to eat these fried worms."
"And why not?"
"You know I like them boiled."

"Now, Junior, be good while I'm away."
"Okay, Pop, I'll be good for a dollar."
"Why, son, when I was your age, I was good for nothing."

MOTHER: He's very kind to animals.
LITTLE SON: Then why doesn't he give his face back to the monkey?

"What are you going to give me for my birthday?"

"Close your eyes and tell me what you
see."

"I see nothing."

"Well, that's what you're going to get!"

"Daddy, why can't I play with the other
kids?"

"Shut up, kid, and deal."

"Aren't you the wonderfully brave young man
who tried to save my son when he fell
through the ice?"

"Yes, ma'am."

"Well, what did you do with his mittens?"

MOTHER: What's the idea of coming home two hours late?
SON (*in bandages*): But, Mom, I was run over.
MOTHER: It doesn't take two hours to get run over.

"I'm sorry, Mrs. Jones, but Johnny was run over by a steamroller."
"I'm in the tub now. Just slip him under the door."

"Mommy, Mommy! The lawn mower just cut off my foot."
"Well, stay outside until it stops bleeding. I just vacuumed the rug."

"Hey, Mom, Junior's on fire!"
"Well, shut off the furnace. There's no point wasting fuel."

"Mom, when will we get a garbage can?"
"Shut up, kid, and keep eating."

"Mommy, what's
a werewolf?"
    "Shut up, kid,
    and comb
    your face."

"But, Mom, I
love to talk."
    "Shut up, kid,
    and drink this
    glue."

"Mommy, why do I keep going around in cir-
cles?"
    "Shut up, kid, or I'll nail your other foot
    to the floor."

"Suzy, for the last time—either you stop
playing with your brother or I shut the cof-
fin."

DOCTOR: Ouch! Ouch!
MOTHER: Now, Junior, please say "ah" so the
    nice doctor can take his finger out of your
    mouth.

I said, "perhaps" and that's final!

"Can Johnny come out and play with us?"
"No, he can't. He caught pneumonia and died three days ago."
"Can we use his sled?"

"Daddy, why can't we have a dog?"
"Shut up, kid, and keep barking."

"Mom, can I lick the beaters on the mixer?"
"Sure, here."
"But, Mom, don't you think you ought to shut off the motor?"

"Ma—Dad was just hit by a car!"
   "Don't make me laugh, son. You know my
   lips are chapped."

"Mommy,   quick,   where   are   the   marsh-
mallows?"
   "Why?"
"Marvin's on fire!"

"I've got a stomach ache."
   "That's because you haven't eaten. Your
   stomach is empty—that's why it hurts."
"Oh, is that why you have all those head-
aches?"

"Mom, can I go out and play?"
   "With those holes in your socks?"
"No, with the kids next door."

14
Shall We Dance?

"May I have the next dance?"
"Of course—this is a charity ball, isn't it?"

JOHN (*handing a chocolate*): Here, honey, sweets to the sweet.

MARY: Oh, thank you. Won't you have some of these nuts?

"I have a tremendous yen for you."
"How much is that in regular money?"

HE: Say something soft and sweet.

SHE: Custard pudding.

"I would go to the ends of the earth for you."
"Yes, but would you stay there?"

"I'll be seeing you."
"Not if I see you first."

Why don't you make like paint—and splatter!

"When I get old and ugly, will you still talk to me?"
    "Don't I?"

"You remind me of the ocean."
    "You mean—because I'm wild and
    romantic?"
"No, because you're all wet."

"Did you miss me
when I was
gone?"
    "Were you
    gone?"

"I thought of you
all day yesterday."
    "Really? Where
    were you?"
"At the zoo."

"Is that perfume I smell?"
    "It is—and you do."

"Are you afraid of the Big Bad Wolf?"
    "Certainly not!"
"That's funny. The other two pigs were."

"You remind me of a vacation from school."

"How is that?"
"No class."

"If you won't marry me, I'll blow my brains out."

"That would be a great joke on Dad. He says you don't have any."

I dreamed about you last night. Worst nightmare I ever had.

"Do you like my company?"

"I don't know. What company are you with?"

"How do you like me as a whole?"
"As a hole you're all right. As a human being—no!"

HE: I love a good old-fashioned girl.
SHE: Come over to my house and I'll introduce you to my grandmother.

HE: You bring out the beast in me.
SHE: I know—a jackass.

HE: I'm looking for a pretty girl.
SHE: Well—here I am!
HE: Swell. You can help me look.

"You remind me of a pie."
"You mean I'm so sweet?"
"No, you have a lot of crust."

"If you were my husband, I'd feed you poison."
"If I were your husband, I'd take it."

I can't remember your name—and please don't bother to tell me.

The only kind of poetry you could think up would be blank verse.

"I got a splinter in my finger."
"You ought to have more sense than to scratch your head."

"You know, I can imitate any bird you can name."
"How about a homing pigeon?"

15
Meanies
but Goodies

The firing squad was escorting a prisoner to his place of execution. It was a dismal, rainy day.

"What a terrible day to die," the condemned man complained.

"What are you kicking about?" the guard said. "We have to walk all the way back in the rain."

"Does anyone on board know how to pray?"
   "I do."
"Good. You pray. The rest of us will put on
life vests. We're one short."

"Shine your shoes, mister?"
   "No."
"Shine your shoes so you can see your face
in them?"
   "I told you no!"
"I don't blame you."

"What is that book
the orchestra leader
keeps looking at?"
   "That's the score."
"Really? Who's
winning?"

BYSTANDER (*at scene of crash*): Have an accident?

VICTIM: No, thanks, I just had one.

"Get some wood for the fire."
  "Sorry, but it's all gone."
"No, it isn't, use your head."

"When I sat down to play the piano, they all laughed."
  "How come?
"No bench."

"You and your suicide attempts! Just look at this gas bill!"

A man came into the doctor's office with two badly burned ears.

"What happened to your ears?" the doctor asked.

"I was ironing my shirt when the phone rang. I accidentally reached for the iron instead of the phone," the man said.

"I could understand if only one of your ears was burned," said the doctor, "but two?"

"Well," came the answer, "the phone rang again."

CUSTOMER: Waiter, have you forgotten me?
WAITER: Oh, no, ma'am, you're the stuffed tomato.

IGOR: Commissar! Commissar! The troops are revolting!

COMMISSAR: Well, you're pretty revolting yourself.

"Will you pass the nuts, teacher?"
"No, I think I'll flunk them."

TEACHER: Johnny, can you tell me what they did at the Boston Tea Party?

JOHNNY: I don't know, Teacher. I wasn't invited.

TEACHER: What's a vacuum, William?
WILLIAM: Wait a minute, Teacher. I have it in my head.

"Can you lend me fifty dollars for a month, old boy?"
    "What would a month-old-boy want with fifty dollars?"

"Did you get the license number of the woman who ran you over?"
    "No, but I'd recognize that laugh anywhere."

CUSTOMER: Give me some cockroach powder.
CLERK: Shall I wrap it up?
CUSTOMER: No, I'll send the roaches down to eat it here.

WANT AD
    Man to work as garbage collector.
    Good salary and all you can eat.

"Hello, Sam's Department Store? Do you have any sleeping bags?"
    "Yes, we do."
"Well, why don't you wake them up?"

"How did you get along with Dad while I
was away, son?"
  "Fine, Mom. Every morning he took me
  down to the lake in a rowboat and let me
  swim back."
"Isn't that a long way to swim?"
  "The swimming wasn't too bad. The hard
  part was getting out of the bag."

WOMAN (*in art gallery*): And this, I suppose,
  is one of those hideous monstrosities you
  call modern art?
ART DEALER: No, madam, it's a mirror.

"Other than that, Mrs. Lincoln, how did you like the play?"

"And how much would you like to contribute to the Indian relief fund, Mrs. Custer?"

"Oh, I wouldn't worry about Nathan, Mrs. Hale. He's probably still hanging around somewhere in the East."

WOMAN (*to trash collector*): Am I too late for the garbage truck?
TRASH COLLECTOR: No, lady, jump right in!

"I went to the zoo yesterday."
"Were you accepted?"

"I don't have an enemy in the world."
"True—only your friends hate you."

He received a sinister note, saying, "Give us $50,000 or you'll never see your wife again."
"I don't have the money," the man replied, "but your proposition interests me."

"What has she got that I don't have?"
"Shall I list it for you alphabetically?"

Read in the will of a miserly millionaire: ". . . and to my dear nephew, Sam, whom I promised I'd remember in my will, 'Hi, there Sam!' "

The businessman lay on his deathbed. "I have a confession to make," he sobbed to his partner. "I robbed our firm of $100,000. I sold our business secrets to our competitors. I stole merchandise. I lied and cheated and—"
    "That's all right, old man," said his partner. "It was me who poisoned you."

Index